NARROW GAUGE RAILWAYS

NORTHUMBERLAND COUNTY LIBRARY

You should return this book on or before the last date stamped below unless an extension of the loan period is granted.

Application for renewal may be made by letter or telephone.

Fines at the approved rate will be charged when a book is overdue.

Published in Great Britain in 2013 by Shire Publications Ltd, Midland House, West Way, Botley, Oxford OX2 0PH, United Kingdom.

43-01 21st Street, Suite 220B, Long Island City, NY 11101, USA.

E-mail: shire@shirebooks.co.uk   www.shirebooks.co.uk

A CIP catalogue record for this book is available from the British Library.

Shire Library no. 772.   ISBN-13: 978 0 74781 297 5

Peter Johnson has asserted his right under the Copyright, Designs and Patents Act, 1988, to be identified as the author of this book.

Designed by Tony Truscott Designs, Sussex, UK and typeset in Perpetua and Gill Sans.

Printed in China through Worldprint Ltd.

13 14 15 16 17   10 9 8 7 6 5 4 3 2 1

COVER IMAGE

High in the Vale of Festiniog, the Festiniog Railway's double Fairlie *David Lloyd George* puts on a show for photographers with a train of vintage stock on the 2-foot gauge line's spiral at Dduallt.

TITLE PAGE IMAGE

Vale of Rheidol Light Railway Davies & Metcalfe 2-6-2T No 1 *Edward VII* at Capel Bangor. Specialising in steam injectors, Davies & Metcalfe built only the two Vale of Rheidol locomotives.

CONTENTS PAGE IMAGE

A feature of the Rheidol valley enjoyed by passengers on the Vale of Rheidol Light Railway is the lead-mine spoil that has poisoned the ground in the shape of a stag.

EDITOR'S NOTE

Locomotives are described by their wheel arrangements and the type of water tank they have, if they have one. An 0-4-0 has no leading wheels, four driving wheels, no trailing wheels and a tender. An 0-4-0T has side tanks on either side of its boiler. Other arrangements mentioned in this book are 0-4-2ST, 0-6-0T, 2-6-2T. Types of tanks used are well tanks (WT), located between the locomotive's frames, and saddle tanks (ST), which sit on top of the boiler. Some Festiniog Railway locomotives have tanks and tenders, 0-4-0STT and 2-4-0STT. The FR's double Fairlies are 0-4-4-0T, its single Fairlie *Taliesin* is 0-4-4T. The Welsh Highland Railway's Garratts are 2-6-2+2-6-2T and 0-4-0+0-4-0T because they have two power units sharing a common boiler. Perform an internet search on 'Whyte notation' for more details.

WELSH PLACE NAMES

Many Welsh places popular with English visitors had or have English versions of their names, and for this reason variations may be found in the text, depending on period and popular usage. During the second half of the twentieth century some of them restored the Welsh version to prominence. Examples are: Betws-y-Coed/Bettws-y-Coed; Carnarvon/Caernarvon/Caernarfon; Cwellyn/Quellyn; Festiniog/Ffestiniog; Portmadoc/Porthmadog; Towyn/Tywyn; Waenfawr/Waunfawr.

IMAGE ACKNOWLEDGEMENTS

G. E. Baddeley, page 12; Brittain & Wright, page 36; R. Carter, page 34; Clay Cross Company, page 61; E. T. W. Dennis, page 28; Frith, page 28; D. George, page 24, 26; Gwenfro, page 32; Kingsway, pages 19, 37, 42; A. McEwing, page 50; R. Morgan, page 30; Moss, page 36; North Staffordshire Railway, page 50; J. S. Peters, page 42; Pictorial Stationery, pages 20, 2, 50; Robin Stewart-Smith, cover image; Valentine, page 49.

All other images are by the author or are in his collection.

Shire Publications is supporting the Woodland Trust, the UK's leading woodland conservation charity, by funding the dedication of trees.

CONTENTS

INTRODUCTION   4

THE FESTINIOG RAILWAY   6

DEVELOPING FESTINIOG CONCEPTS   16

WIDER DOES NOT NECESSARILY MEAN BIGGER   24

3-FOOT GAUGE   34

THE LIGHT RAILWAYS   40

BETWEEN THE WARS:
A NARROW GAUGE SWANSONG   53

PLACES TO VISIT   62

FURTHER READING   63

INDEX   64

INTRODUCTION

Cnicht, known as the 'Welsh Matterhorn' in Victorian times, dominates the view as this Welsh Highland Railway train approaches Porthmadog on its journey from Caernarfon.

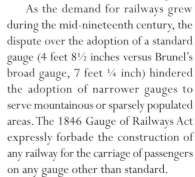

Narrow gauge railways, where the rails are closer together than those used on main lines, were first used in mines and quarries, where the tracks could reach into confined spaces and the wagons were small enough to be pushed by men or pulled by ponies. They were cheaper to build, cuttings and embankments were smaller, and curves could be sharper so they could follow the contours of the land more easily. In industry these railways could be very short: sometimes as little as 100 feet long.

As the demand for railways grew during the mid-nineteenth century, the dispute over the adoption of a standard gauge (4 feet 8½ inches versus Brunel's broad gauge, 7 feet ¼ inch) hindered the adoption of narrower gauges to serve mountainous or sparsely populated areas. The 1846 Gauge of Railways Act expressly forbade the construction of any railway for the carriage of passengers on any gauge other than standard.

The realisation that standard gauge could not meet all requirements brought some measure of relaxation to its mandated use, however. In Wales, the spiritual home of narrow gauge railways, the Talyllyn Railway's 1865 Act was the first to permit a sub-standard gauge (2 feet 3 inches) for the carriage of passengers, and the Festiniog Railway, further north, became the first narrow gauge railway to carry them officially. The Festiniog Railway's success – which occurred mainly because it had a

4

monopoly of the slate traffic, not just because it was cheap to build and operate – was responsible for the evangelical promotion of narrow gauge railways around the world.

There was no standard narrow gauge: there was originally no need for one. The variants around 2 feet usually had their origins in man- or animal-worked tramways in mines or quarries, while engineers were to conclude that a gauge of 2 feet 6 inches or 3 feet struck a better balance between the cost of construction and capacity.

Narrow gauge should not be considered synonymous with small, for capacity is a factor of loading gauge (the maximum size that rolling stock can be in order to get through tunnels and bridges safely), rather than the gauge of the tracks themselves: the 2-foot-gauge Festiniog Railway stock is larger than that of the 2-foot 3-inch-gauge Talyllyn Railway; and the 2-foot-gauge stock in use on the Welsh Highland Railway is too large for the Festiniog. Regardless of their gauge, railways in the United Kingdom required an Act of Parliament or a Light Railway Order before they could carry passengers. Exceptions were those built on private property, like the 2-foot 7½-inch-gauge Snowdon Mountain Railway or the 3-foot-gauge Rye & Camber Tramway.

Few narrow gauge railways made any money for their shareholders, and to a greater or lesser extent they all suffered in the Depression after the First World War, and from competition from motor transport; few of them outlasted the 1930s. The Talyllyn Railway was one of those that did, but it was badly run down. At a time when many traditional industries were struggling to survive, the threat to the Talyllyn Railway when its owner died in 1950 was sufficient to set in motion the events that led to its preservation and the establishment of the railway preservation movement.

Since 1951 most of these narrow gauge railways have found new lives carrying tourists. Their success has encouraged both the construction of new railways to serve parks and zoos and the adaptation of disused standard gauge railway trackbeds for new narrow gauge lines. Some individuals have even built narrow gauge railways in farms or gardens for their own amusement. The restricted space available in this book, however, allows only the 'classic' narrow gauge passenger-carrying railways – 2-foot gauge and greater – which existed before 1951, to be covered.

Poster published after Henry Haydn Jones took over the Bryneglwys slate quarries and the Talyllyn Railway in 1911. A blank was left in the date so that it could be used in any year. Another, similar, poster was issued in the 1920s.

THE FESTINIOG RAILWAY

THE FESTINIOG RAILWAY is the pre-eminent narrow gauge railway. It gained – and has maintained – an international reputation for innovation, particularly in its use of articulated locomotives and bogie carriages. Built under an 1832 statute and opened in 1836, its function was the carriage of slate from quarries at Blaenau Ffestiniog, in the old county of Merioneth, to the harbour at Port Madock (now Porthmadog, via Portmadoc), in Carnarvonshire, a distance of 13¼ miles. It is the oldest un-amalgamated railway company in the world. Its name was given to it by Act of Parliament at a time when spellings nof Welsh place names had not been standardised and when English versions were often used. Today, for marketing purposes, the form 'Ffestiniog Railway' is usually used. The original spelling is used in this book.

Construction of mills and workers' houses that accompanied the Industrial Revolution created a huge demand for roofing slate. Before the railway, pack animals had carried the slate to wharves on the river Dwyryd, where it was transhipped into river craft for carriage to coastal shipping in deeper water. Use of the river limited the time when slate could be shipped to the spring tides, in alternate weeks, when the weather was fine. The 13s 3d per ton that it cost to transport the slate to the sea was almost double the cost of production, and if it were bound for London then it would cost an additional £1 per ton.

The railway was built at the instigation of quarry owner Samuel Holland and Dublin businessman Henry Archer. The route was surveyed by James Spooner and he and Archer supervised construction. Over the 13¼ miles the railway descended 720 feet to the port, with an average gradient of 1 in 79, which enabled loaded wagons to descend by gravity. Horses were used to haul the empty wagons back to the quarries.

The gauge is 1 foot 11½ inches, but 2 feet is convenient shorthand. Features of the line were the use of dry-stone embankments, to reduce the amount of land required, and routing it along the top of the embankment across the mouth of the river Glaslyn. William Alexander Madocks, the MP

Opposite:
Double Fairlie
Merddin Emrys
(built in 1879)
and a vintage train
on a quiet
October day
at Tan y Bwlch,
7½ miles from
Porthmadog.

The replica Lynton & Barnstaple Railway Manning, Wardle 2-6-2T *Lyd* crosses the Cei Mawr, the Festiniog Railway's largest dry-stone embankment.

for Boston, Lincolnshire, and owner of property on the Glaslyn estuary, had built the embankment (nearly a mile long, and completed in 1812) to reclaim estuarial land. Cei Mawr embankment, 4½ miles from Porthmadog, is 62 feet high, the largest of its type in Europe.

At the inland end, branches to Rhiwbryfdir and Duffws targeted the main slate quarries, although initially Holland was the only quarry owner to use the line. Despite the railway charging only 6s per ton, it was 1839 before the others started to make the investment required to connect to it.

Gravity trains comprised six to eight wagons and ran at 10 mph, terminating at the Boston Lodge weighbridge at the Merionethshire end of the embankment. After sorting, horses pulled the wagons across to the harbour. With increasing traffic and experience, both the speed and the length of the gravity trains increased.

The railway was profitable from 1843. In addition to paying dividends, its revenue was sufficient to pay for substantial improvements to the track and alignment. A 730-yard-long tunnel to replace Archer's inclines over a spur of the Moelwyns was completed in 1842. The shorter 60-yard tunnel at Garnedd, half a mile from Tan y Bwlch, was built in 1851. Growing traffic increased train length but there were limitations on capacity; longer trains required more horses, increasing costs. The first of six locomotives built by George England of Hatcham, London, was delivered in July 1863; within two years costs had been reduced by 22 per cent.

The first passenger carriages were delivered in 1864 and Captain Henry Whatley Tyler inspected the line for the Board of Trade in October, making several recommendations, including the locking of carriage doors (due to the limited clearances). Public passenger service was operated from 5 January 1865. Two bogie carriages obtained in 1872 were probably the first of the type to be used in the United Kingdom and both are still in use.

Seen near Rhiw Goch with the Moelwyns in the background, the Festiniog Railway's gravity train heads towards Porthmadog.

Little Wonder,
the first of the
Festiniog Railway's
double Fairlie
locomotives,
was photographed
with four-wheeled
carriages and the
first-generation
quarrymen's train
at Tan y Bwlch.
Understandably,
the quarrymen
demanded better
accommodation
but the company
was never very
generous with
what it gave them.

The engineer Robert Francis Fairlie had offered to supply one of his newly patented articulated locomotives in 1869. Delivered in July and named *Little Wonder*, it had a double boiler and two four-wheeled power bogies. It proved to have more than twice the hauling capacity of the existing locomotives and soon proved its worth. Although Fairlie locomotives were used around the world, they came to be particularly associated with the Festiniog Railway.

The company's profitability brought it under fire from two directions: from the quarry owners, who thought that their rates should be reduced; and from other railways, who wanted a share of the business. The slate rate included the supply of wagons, which were used unofficially for storage in the quarries and on the wharves, leading to complaints about shortages.

The exchange yard with the Cambrian Railways at Minffordd was opened in 1874 and the London & North Western and Great Western Railways opened branch lines to Blaenau Ffestiniog in 1881 and 1883 respectively. The GWR had taken over and converted the 2-foot gauge 3½-mile-long Ffestiniog & Blaenau Railway, which had connected with the FR at Dolgarreg

Ddu in Blaenau Ffestiniog from 1868, incorporating it into its route from Bala. As well as passengers, the FBR had fed the FR with slate from Craig Ddu quarry. This traffic continued under GWR auspices, the narrow gauge wagons being carried on standard gauge transporter wagons.

The LNWR undercut the FR rates, triggering a gradual decline in its profitability. Before the impact of competition was felt too deeply, however, the FR did experience some good years, having the confidence to build two Fairlie locomotives, *Merddin Emrys* (1879) and *Livingston Thompson* (1886). But by the time war broke out in 1914 it had not paid any dividends for several years.

The Festiniog Railway was the only narrow gauge railway to be placed under Government control for the duration of the war, as the mainline companies had been. This had little effect from an operating perspective but the Government controlled revenue and expenditure. By the time control was handed back in 1920, the FR had an unauthorised £6,000 overdraft, the maintenance was in arrears and the Government's compensation was insufficient to restore the pre-war status quo.

The Welsh Highland Railway promoters acquired control of the company in 1922 and in 1923 the two railways were connected at Porthmadog. There was some interchange of rolling stock between them. Colonel Holman Fred Stephens, who had gained a reputation for managing light railways, was employed as engineer of both lines in 1923 and became a director and then Chairman in 1924. His involvement influenced the acquisition of two petrol-engined locomotives and several wagons that had been made for wartime service. Six semi-open carriages were bought as well.

During the inter-war years, industrial disputes, foreign competition and the availability of new roofing materials combined to reduce the slate traffic. Motor buses, set up in competition, took the local passenger traffic and from 1930 the passenger service became seasonal, for the benefit of the growing tourist traffic. Before long it was subsidising the remaining slate traffic. From 1934 the FR leased the unsuccessful Welsh Highland Railway.

The outbreak of war in September 1939 brought an end to the passenger service. Slate trains continued to run as required until

A popular sight on the Festiniog Railway in the 1930s, Bessie Jones lived at the Tan y Bwlch station house and was allowed to offer refreshments to passengers. She posed for many photographs and sold picture postcards of herself.

In 1863, 0-4-0STT *Prince* was the fourth steam locomotive delivered to the Festiniog Railway. Nearly a century later, in 1955, it was the first to be restored for use on the revived railway.

A classic Festiniog Railway scene at Tan y Bwlch. The trains include both of the first two-bogie carriages and two of the distinctive brake vans with the 'curly' roof.

1946, when, without the funds needed to restore the line to carry passengers, it was closed. The 650 yards between Duffws and the former LNWR yard in Blaenau Ffestiniog were leased to the quarries.

Several approaches were made to the company with proposals for the railway's preservation. The one that succeeded, in 1950, was started by Leonard Heath Humphrys, a fifteen-year-old schoolboy, but it took until June 1954 to find a way to acquire control of the company and to settle the overdraft.

Businessman Alan Pegler was a railway enthusiast. Friends had told him about the FR and his father lent him the £3,000 required to buy the majority shareholding. With the support of volunteers provided by the newly formed Festiniog Railway Society, the track across Madocks's embankment was fettled and brought into use on 23 July 1955.

The response from tourists was encouraging and services were extended to Minffordd (2 miles) in 1956, Penrhyn (3 miles) in 1957, and Tan y Bwlch

The spiral on the Festiniog Railway's deviation at Dduallt is unique on a passenger railway in the United Kingdom. Most of its formation was built by volunteers. The line from Porthmadog is at the top of the picture.

(7½ miles) in 1958. A great deal of effort was required to refurbish the overgrown track and to restore locomotives and carriages to carry increasing numbers of passengers.

Progress beyond Tan y Bwlch was hampered by the pumped storage power station that had been built at Tanygrisiau, the lower reservoir flooding the line beyond the Moelwyn tunnel. The compensation claim took thirteen years to settle, but in the meantime volunteers started building a 2½-mile deviation route in 1965. After ten years of consolidation, the services were extended to Dduallt (9½ miles). Despite the initial scepticism of the power station's owner, the Central Electricity Generating Board, and with the later support of grants from the Wales Tourist Board and the Manpower Services Commission, the deviation, which included construction of a spiral, to gain height, and a 287-yard-long tunnel, was completed to Tanygrisiau (12 miles) in 1978.

Restoration of the line to Blaenau Ffestiniog (14 miles) was completed in 1982. The new terminal station was shared with British Railways. Clearance of the derelict site was partially funded by a forerunner of the European Union, the European Economic Community.

As the Festiniog Railway's original rolling stock was insufficient to accommodate the increasing passenger numbers during the 1960s, before

Double Fairlie *David Lloyd George* arrives at Minffordd, 2 miles from the Festiniog Railway's Porthmadog terminus.

cheap overseas holidays became available to the masses, new carriages were built at Boston Lodge. Several locomotives were obtained, including two 1893-built Hunslet 0-4-0STs from the Penrhyn quarry railway. In 1979 a new double Fairlie, *Earl of Merioneth*, was completed at Boston Lodge, followed by another, *David Lloyd George*, in 1992, single Fairlie *Taliesin* in 1999 and Lynton & Barnstaple Railway Manning, Wardle 2-6-2T *Lyd* in 2010. The last two were funded by supporters, who paid a monthly subscription.

Construction of *David Lloyd George* was supported by a grant, helping the railway to increase its capacity and extend its operating season. Three new carriages fitted out to a high standard, including heating, and the upgrading of three others to the same specification were included in the package. Several more new carriages that meet ever-increasing standards have since been added to the fleet.

From 1990 the Festiniog Railway pursued the restoration of the Welsh Highland Railway, silencing critics and objectors only when it demonstrated its determination to complete the 25-mile line through the Snowdonia National Park. Since 2011 both railways have shared the same station at Porthmadog.

Commemorating the thirtieth anniversary of the restoration of Festiniog Railway services to Blaenau Ffestiniog in 2012, arrangements were made for the trains on standard and narrow gauge to arrive simultaneously. The FR train is hauled by the *Earl of Merioneth*.

DEVELOPING FESTINIOG CONCEPTS

Some twenty-three years apart, two Acts of Parliament produced two very different 2-foot-gauge railways: one in North Wales and the other in Devon.

NORTH WALES NARROW GAUGE RAILWAYS

Charles Easton Spooner, the Festiniog Railway's secretary and engineer, was convinced that the FR model could be replicated elsewhere, not realising that the FR would be so successful only while it had a monopoly on the main traffic.

Nevertheless, with Spooner as its engineer, the North Wales Narrow Gauge Railways obtained an Act of Parliament in 1872. Two undertakings were authorised, from Dinas, 3 miles from Caernarfon, to Bryngwyn (6 miles) with a branch from Tryfan Junction to Rhyd Ddu, at the foot of Snowdon, another 6 miles – the Moel Tryfan Undertaking. The General Undertaking was a route from Porthmadog to Betws-y-Coed via Beddgelert. The main traffic was expected to be slate and other minerals, but passengers were to be accommodated as well.

With funding always a problem, only the Moel Tryfan Undertaking was built, opening to Bryngwyn and Quellyn in 1877, to Snowdon Ranger in 1878 and Rhyd Ddu in 1881. The line climbed 3 miles at 1 in 40 from Dinas to Tryfan Junction before finding a slightly easier way to Rhyd Ddu, 600 feet above sea level. The Bryngwyn branch climbed at up to 1 in 39 before terminating at the foot of the incline, 650 feet, which connected the railway with several slate quarries. The railway-owned incline rose 245 feet over a distance of half a mile.

Although Spooner ended his connection with the railway before it was opened, his influence may be detected in the requirement to adopt Fairlie's patent locomotives for its mainline services. Vulcan Foundry built two of these with the 0-6-4T configuration in 1875, and a Hunslet 0-6-4ST shunting locomotive named *Beddgelert* was obtained in 1878.

The company being unable to meet the payments on the rolling stock, a group of shareholders, led by a London barrister named James Cholmeley

Opposite:
The North Wales Narrow Gauge Railways route between Dinas and Rhyd Ddu has been restored as a part of the Welsh Highland Railway. Several of these distinctive overbridges required underpinning to accommodate the higher modern locomotives and carriages.

Russell, established the Moel Tryfan Rolling Stock Company to purchase it and lease it back to the company. Russell was appointed as receiver when his company put the railway into receivership.

Under his control, the railway just managed to cover its costs but never made enough to pay a dividend. Its best years came after 1893, when Rhyd Ddu station was renamed Snowdon, leading to a big boost in passenger traffic and the funds to buy several new carriages. The effect on tourism in Llanberis, on the other side of the mountain, was responsible for the development of the Snowdon Mountain Railway. After that line was opened for the second time in 1897, the North Wales Narrow Gauge Railways' traffic settled into a steady decline.

In the twentieth century, the North Wales Power Company-sponsored Portmadoc, Beddgelert & South Snowdon Railway promised great things

A North Wales Narrow Gauge Railways train stands at Rhyd Ddu before returning to Dinas. A box of Tate's cube sugar is on the ground next to the locomotive.

for narrow gauge railways in Snowdonia, obtaining authorisation to build 2-foot-gauge electric lines from Porthmadog to Betws-y-Coed via Beddgelert and to Rhyd Ddu. It agreed to electrify the North Wales Narrow Gauge Railways and to work them in perpetuity but when the agreed schedule fell behind in 1906 Russell persuaded the power company to provide a new steam locomotive to replace the worn-out Hunslet *Beddgelert*. The new machine, a Hunslet 2-6-2T, was named *Russell*.

The small surpluses that were made over the years were inadequate to pay dividends or debt repayments, and were held under court supervision; in 1907 and 1908, however, they were released to fund the purchase of two composite brake carriages and another single Fairlie, named *Gowrie*.

By 1914 and the outbreak of the First World War, the railway was in very poor condition. An enthusiast who visited reported seeing daylight through the sides of his carriage. The passenger service ended in 1916. To keep the goods service going, in 1917 the original Fairlies were combined to make a single locomotive, and *Gowrie* was sold.

In 1920 the controlling interest in the railway was transferred to Sir John Henderson Stewart Bt. He appears to have been acting as a nominee for the Aluminium Corporation, which had acquired the North Wales Power Company in 1918. The way was then set for the North Wales Narrow Gauge Railways to become a part of the Welsh Highland Railway.

A button from a Lynton & Barnstaple Railway uniform.

LYNTON & BARNSTAPLE RAILWAY

In Devon, the Lynton & Barnstaple Railway was quite a contrast to the North Wales Narrow Gauge Railways, despite sharing the same gauge. For one thing, it was fully funded and properly resourced to deal with the traffic on offer.

A Lynton & Barnstaple Railway train at Barnstaple in the days of its independence. Here traffic was exchanged with the London & South Western Railway's Ilfracombe line.

The Lynton &
Barnstaple Railway
was noted for its
stylish, chalet-type,
station buildings,
as seen here
at Lynton.

Chelfham viaduct
was the most
imposing structure
on the Lynton &
Barnstaple Railway
and has been
restored by its
original builders.

Authorised by an 1895 Act of Parliament and opened in 1898, it followed a sinuous 19¼-mile route across Exmoor from the market town of Barnstaple to serve the twin coastal resorts of Lynton and Lynmouth. Its principal shareholder and Chairman was the publisher Sir George Newnes, who

One of the Lynton & Barnstaple Railway's original locomotives, *Yeo*, and the Southern Railway's addition to the fleet, *Lew* (leading), at Barnstaple on the railway's last day of operation, 29 September 1935. The design of the Ffestiniog Railway-based Manning, Wardle 2-6-2T *Lyd* (Pages 22–3) is based on *Lew*.

owned property in Lynton. At Barnstaple, there was a cross-platform interchange with the London & South Western Railway. Gradients as steep as 1 in 50 were required to reach the summit (1,000 feet) at Woody Bay before falling to 700 feet at Lynton. The most notable feature was an eight-arch brick viaduct at Chelfham, 70 feet high.

Manning, Wardle supplied three 2-6-2Ts, named *Exe*, *Taw* and *Yeo* after local rivers. In 1898 an American company, Baldwin Locomotive Works, supplied a 2-4-2T named *Lyn*, in kit form, which was assembled by railway personnel in Barnstaple. Bristol Carriage & Wagon supplied sixteen handsome bogie carriages, arguably the best supplied to any narrow gauge railway up to that time. Only mixed trains (passenger and goods) were operated.

The maximum load for the locomotives was four carriages; heavier loads required double heading, so the railway was expensive to operate at peak times. Factors such as this, and the distance of stations from the communities they served, have led to questions being asked about the promoters' intentions: did they perhaps seek to control the number of visitors to 'their' part of Devon?

Lynton & Barnstaple Railway carriage No 15, seen at Snapper after the auction, was acquired and rebuilt by the Festiniog Railway.

At the railway grouping in 1923, the LBR was absorbed into the Southern Railway. A programme of improvements to infrastructure and rolling stock was put in place and a new Manning, Wardle 2-6-2T, *Lew*, was obtained in 1925. The 1920s Depression and increased availability of motor transport affected traffic and the railway was closed in 1935. Large crowds turned out to watch or ride on the last trains. The railway was soon dismantled and

equipment surplus to the Southern's requirements was sold at auction, the land being sold piecemeal in 1938.

In 1979 the Lynton & Barnstaple Railway Association (which became a charitable trust in 2000) was formed with the objective of restoring the railway, although in places the route is blocked by developments including a reservoir. Woody Bay station was purchased in 1995 and the short passenger railway that opened there in 2004 was extended to Killington Lane in 2006, a distance of about a mile. Plans to extend the line to serve a transport hub at Blackmoor Gate are being developed.

Several original carriages and vans survived locally and some remain in existence. Carriage No 2 is displayed at the National Railway Museum, York, and No 15 was rebuilt by the Festiniog Railway as buffet car No 14. Van No 23 has been restored by the Association and carriages Nos 7 and 17 are being restored. Construction of a replica Manning, Wardle 2-6-2T, *Lyd*, was completed at the Festiniog Railway's Boston Lodge works in 2009. In company with carriage Nos 14 and 15, it visited the Lynton & Barnstaple Railway at Woody Bay in September 2010. Another Manning, Wardle and a Baldwin 2-4-2T are also under construction.

With the Bristol Channel visible on the horizon, the Festiniog Railway-based Manning, Wardle 2-6-2T *Lyd* hauls the rebuilt Lynton & Barnstaple Railway carriage, originally No 15, and an FR observation carriage up to Woody Bay in 2011.

Lynton &
Barnstaple Railway
0-6-0T *Axe* at
Woody Bay station
on a summer's
afternoon.

WIDER DOES NOT NECESSARILY MEAN BIGGER

THREE RAILWAYS in Wales and one in Scotland used gauges between 2 feet and 2 feet 6 inches, and all were predominantly used for the transportation of minerals. The Scottish line, the Campbeltown & Machrihanish Light Railway, is discussed on page 51, but the Welsh railways are described here.

CORRIS RAILWAY

The oldest of these lines, the 2-foot 3-inch-gauge Corris and Talyllyn Railways, were quite close together on the borders of Merionethshire and Montgomeryshire. The first was opened as the Corris, Machynlleth & River Dovey Tramroad in 1859, pursuant to a series of Acts of Parliament enacted between 1852 and 1858. Serving slate quarries at Aberllefenni, it ran down the Dulas valley to reach wharves on the banks of the Dyfi (then Dovey), at Morben and Derwenlas near the market town of Machynlleth, a distance of 7½ miles. There was a branch line to more quarries at Upper Corris. In common with the Festiniog Railway, loaded trains were worked by gravity, with horses returning the empty wagons to the quarries.

Around 1863–4 the railway was acquired by the contractor Thomas Savin, who tried to sell it to the Aberystwyth & Welsh Coast Railway. When this line was opened in 1863 the Corris line to the wharves fell out of use. The railway's name became 'Corris Railway' in an 1864 Act, when power to use steam locomotives was obtained. Savin's bankruptcy in 1866 put the railway into limbo until it was sold to the Tramways & General Works Company and then to Imperial Tramways in 1878. An agreement was made for the first to reconstruct and equip the railway for locomotive working and passenger carrying. Although the carriage of passengers was expressly forbidden by the railway's 1864 Act, it is probable that passengers had been carried unofficially since the railway opened; from 1874 until 1879, when the practice stopped, the numbers carried were included in official returns. One of the quarry owners objected to the carriage of passengers on the grounds that it would interfere with the slate traffic, but another Act gave permission in 1880. When the inspecting officer attended in October,

Opposite:
The photographer has persuaded this Corris Railway train crew to pose with their locomotive on the river bridge at Corris. A second bridge behind it carries the road.

Above: A Corris Railway stamp issued as a receipt for the payment due for the carriage of newspapers.

Above right: A train of seven bogie carriages and a van hauled by two locomotives pauses for the photographer on the Corris Railway Dyfi river bridge, near Machynlleth. How often the railway's engineer's ban on double-heading was ignored is not known.

however, he refused to approve the railway's use by passengers because it was partly built beyond the limits of deviation: the curves were too sharp and the clearances were too tight.

It took three years, and another Act, before the railway obtained the Board of Trade's approval to carry passengers on the 5-mile stretch between Machynlleth and Corris. Tramways & General Works had supplied the railway with three Hughes 0-4-0STs and eight four-wheeled tramway-style carriages. The limited clearances were dealt with by allowing access to the trains from only one side. From 1888 the Railway started a programme of improving its carriage stock by buying bogie carriages and by mounting pairs of original carriages on to bogie underframes. The locomotives were improved by the addition of trailing pony trucks, a pair of wheels articulated to the locomotive frames that improves the quality of its ride and takes some of its weight.

During its horse and gravity days the railway had been very profitable. The increased costs associated with steam traction reduced its profitability considerably and it was subsidised by Imperial Tramways. Tourism was an essential part of the railway's business and it ran horse buses from Corris to Talyllyn in connection with the trains.

Some significant investments were made in the twentieth century. Machynlleth station was replaced in 1904/5, the Dyfi river bridge was renewed in 1906 and a Kerr, Stuart 'Tattoo' 0-4-2ST was purchased in 1921. Charabancs had been used on the road service since 1910 and the routes expanded to cover Aberystwyth, Dolgellau and Abergynolwyn as well as Talyllyn.

The Great Western Railway's purchase of the line for £1,000 in 1929 had been a condition of a transaction to purchase the Bristol Tramways & Carriage Company, a company that had links to Imperial Tramways. The most obvious change to the railway was the withdrawal of passenger services from 1 January 1931, when two of the carriages were sold to owners in Gobowen for use as sheds; the remainder were scrapped.

The railway survived until August 1948, just after it had been nationalised. At this time, heavy rain threatened to undermine the Dyfi river bridge and the traffic did not justify the cost of repair. The track was dismantled by 1951 and the two remaining locomotives were kept in store at Machynlleth until they were sold to the Talyllyn Railway in 1951.

Moves to preserve and restore the railway followed the establishment of a society in 1966. Four years later, a museum was opened in Corris, and in 2002 a train service was started between Corris and the original locomotive

Opposite, bottom: A Corris Railway train at Machynlleth. The bogie carriages show differences in detail between them.

Corris Railway No 7, a Kerr, Stuart 'Tattoo' 0-4-2ST that entered service in 2005, photographed at the railway's Maespoeth depot. The locomotive supplied to the railway in 1921 is preserved on the Talyllyn Railway.

shed at Maespoeth, just under a mile. In 2005 a new Kerr, Stuart 'Tattoo' 0-4-2ST was commissioned. Plans to extend southwards to Tan y Coed, near Esgairgeiliog, are being developed and a Hughes 0-4-2ST is under construction.

Opposite page: Tree growth over 150 years conceals this view of a Talyllyn Railway train on Dolgoch viaduct. The locomotive is Fletcher, Jennings 0-4-0WT *Dolgoch*.

Left: The Talyllyn Railway's first locomotive, Fletcher, Jennings 0-4-2ST *Tal-y-llyn*, was looking a bit battered when photographed at the turn of the twentieth century.

TALYLLYN RAILWAY

About 4 miles away, the Bryn Eglwys quarries tapped the same slate veins as those worked in the Corris area. From 1866, however, their slate was exported to a wharf on the Cambrian Railways' line on the Cardigan Bay coast at Tywyn via the Talyllyn Railway, which was also 2-foot 3-inch gauge. The quarry company owned the railway company.

The route was surveyed in 1864 by James Swinton Spooner, a son of the Festiniog Railway's Charles Easton Spooner, and construction was started soon afterwards, an Act of Parliament having been obtained in 1865. With an inland terminus at Abergynolwyn, 242 feet above sea level, the line

The abandoned trackbed of the Corris Railway between Corris and Aberllefenni.

was 6½ miles long. The quarries were connected by inclines and a mineral siding. An incline down from the siding enabled heavier goods to be delivered to the village, which was about half a mile from the station. The steepest gradient is a short stretch of 1 in 69 at Ty Mawr. At Dolgoch, a 51-foot-high, three-arch viaduct crosses a ravine.

The Cumbrian firm of Fletcher, Jennings supplied the railway with two locomotives of very different appearance: an 0-4-0ST in 1864 and an 0-4-0WT in 1866, named *Tal-y-llyn* and *Dolgoch* respectively. The first was soon modified to 0-4-2ST to improve its stability. Four four-wheeled carriages and a van provided the passenger accommodation. An unusual feature of the van was the inclusion of a booking office window for the sale of tickets at intermediate stations. Another carriage was obtained in 1870.

Inclines were a feature of many narrow gauge railways, usually for the export of minerals from quarries. The Talyllyn Railway's Abergynolwyn village incline was an exception, provided to deliver merchandise and to remove 'night soil'.

Goods services started as soon as construction allowed, with passenger services following in December 1866. The government inspector had refused to approve them because clearances through the overbridges were too tight. This was resolved by moving the track over to one side and screwing the carriage doors closed on that side.

The quarries and their railway were not the busiest in Wales and no other rolling stock was required. In 1911 they were purchased by the local MP, Henry Haydn Jones, as a personal job creation/maintenance scheme and he kept them going until his death in 1950. In 1935 he also took a seven-year lease on the Aberllefenni slate quarry to keep the Corris Railway open.

A view of the Talyllyn Railway's Tywyn terminus in about 1963. The train about to depart, hauled by the former Corris Railway Kerr, Stuart 'Tattoo' 0-4-2ST, includes the two former Glyn Valley Tramway carriages, painted green, and two former Penrhyn quarrymen's carriages. The 3-foot 4-inch-gauge Corpet 0-6-0T *Cambrai*, which had been used in the Leicestershire iron ore industry, is on display outside the original Narrow Gauge Railway Museum.

After Jones's death, writer and historian Tom Rolt and his friends persuaded his executors to hand over the railway to the newly formed Talyllyn Railway Preservation Society. On 14 May 1951 it was run with the support of volunteers, the first to be preserved in the world. Public response was good, encouraging the team to make the effort required to overcome the ravages of time on the original rolling stock and rail that was still in use. Everything was extremely worn out and needed to be repaired and replaced in the interest of safety, but over the next forty years new locomotives and carriages were acquired, built and restored. The most notable

A contrasting view some forty years later. The train engine is Fletcher, Jennings 0-4-0WT *Dolgoch*, built for the railway in 1866.

acquisitions were two locomotives, one bogie carriage and several wagons formerly used on the Corris Railway, and two Glyn Valley Tramway carriages.

Facilities throughout the railway were improved and in 1976, after six years' work, the railway was extended by ¾ mile over the mineral line to a new station at Nant Gwernol. A substantial new station at Tywyn was opened by their Royal Highnesses the Prince of Wales and the Duchess of Cornwall in 2005, accommodating the Narrow Gauge Railway Museum as well as the booking hall, shop and café. Under-cover storage at Pendre works was supplemented by a new stock shed at Quarry Siding in 2012.

Traffic peaked at 100,000 passengers in 1973 and 1978 before falling back to around 45,000; it will be a significant challenge for the railway and its supporters to keep this historic line going.

GLYN VALLEY TRAMWAY

Located on the England / Wales border, about 60 miles from Tywyn, was the 2-foot 4-inch-gauge Glyn Valley Tramway, which ran 6 miles between Chirk and Glyn Ceiriog, in Denbighshire. It was opened in 1873 for the carriage of goods and minerals, including slate and granite, and in 1874 for passengers. At Chirk, traffic was exchanged with the Great Western Railway or the Shropshire Union Canal. Haulage was initially by horses, with passengers riding in wagons before three four-wheeled carriages were put into service.

The route was a roadside tramway, which placed limitations on the use of steam locomotives. Starting in 1887, the line was rebuilt to make it suitable. In 1888 goods haulage started using two 0-4-2T tram engines obtained from Beyer, Peacock; they had their motion concealed to reduce the risk of frightening livestock on the road. After a five-year interval, passenger services were resumed

The Glyn Valley Tramway's passenger terminus at Glyn Ceiriog.

Dennis, one of the Glyn Valley Tramway's Beyer, Peacock tram engines, hauled the first steam passenger service on the line in 1891. It was seen at Chirk thirty-one years later.

in 1891, and fourteen more four-wheeled carriages were purchased over the next ten years. A third tram engine was obtained in 1892 and in 1921 an ex-War Department Baldwin 4-6-0PT was re-gauged from 2 feet and put into service.

The inter-war Depression and increased use of motor vehicles finished the passenger traffic in 1933 and the goods traffic ended two years later. The locomotives were scrapped and the carriages sold for non-rail use locally; two were to be obtained and restored by the Talyllyn Railway in the 1950s.

Two organisations with different objectives have taken an interest in the tramway and its remains. In 2012 one of them obtained planning permission to construct a railway on the short section between Chirk and Pontfaen.

Photographed inside the locomotive shed at Chirk are the Glyn Valley Tramway's Baldwin 4-6-0PT and Beyer, Peacock tram engine *Sir Theodore*.

3-FOOT GAUGE

THE USE of 3-foot gauge on the UK mainland was unusual, only two public lines being built in England, on opposite coasts. Another coastal 3-foot-gauge line, the Rye & Camber Tramway, was built without statutory authority, and the Aluminium Corporation had an extensive 3-foot-gauge system serving its works near Fort William. Much greater use was made of this gauge in the Isle of Man and in Ireland.

RAVENGLASS & ESKDALE RAILWAY

The Ravenglass & Eskdale Railway was opened from an interchange with the Furness Railway on the Cumbrian coast at Ravenglass and ran 7 miles eastwards, terminating at Boot. It was promoted by the Whitehaven Iron Mines Company, which owned one of several iron ore mines located near Boot. Authorised by an 1873 Act of Parliament, it was opened in 1875, equipped with just one Manning, Wardle 0-6-0T.

In 1876 Manning, Wardle supplied a second locomotive, and two passenger carriages and a brake van were obtained from the Bristol Wagon Company. A third carriage was built locally. All were four-wheeled. The passenger service was started on 20 November 1876.

Being unable to pay the contractor and evidently unable to place the £12,000 additional capital authorised by the Board of Trade in March 1876, the railway was placed in receivership in 1877. Mineral traffic peaked at 9,138 tons in that year and, following the collapse of one of the mining companies, had fallen to less than 1,000 tons ten years later. Passenger traffic, on the other hand, grew to 21,733 by 1880 and generally ranged between 20,000 and 30,000 thereafter. It was insufficient to offset the loss of the mineral traffic, however.

Remaining in receivership, the railway struggled: its stock was ill-maintained and decrepit. A proposal for the Furness Railway to take over its operation in 1898 came to nothing, and by the end of the 1908 season the railway was in such a poor condition that it was closed. In 1909 powers were obtained to create a new company to take over the assets of the old and to

Opposite:
Many narrow gauge railways, and a few standard gauge ones, gained a reputation for haphazard operations. Southwold artist Reg Carter produced sixteen postcards representing his local line.

A Ravenglass & Eskdale Railway train leaves Boot with all the railway's passenger stock. The carriage next to the locomotive was built by the railway for use at busy times.

The 1844 Regulation of Railways Act required railways to run at least one train daily with covered carriages at a speed of not less than 12 mph and a fare of not more than 1d per mile, for the benefit of workers. Special tickets were issued. The journey represented by this ticket took five minutes.

Ravenglass & Eskdale Railway.
BOOT
TO
BECKFOOT
PARLIAMENTARY.
Issued subject to the Regulations & Conditions contained in the Co's Time Bills.

raise funds to reconstruct the railway for passenger traffic. Before they came into effect one of the quarries took a six-month lease on the line. When it expired at the end of the year the Eskdale Railway Company took over. Despite the optimism, no fresh capital was forthcoming and the railway was not rebuilt.

Trains were run by the company in 1910; in 1911 it was leased again and thereafter was worked spasmodically, dependent on the stone available, but from 30 April 1913 it was abandoned.

In 1915 it was taken over by Narrow Gauge Railways Ltd as a vehicle for the rail products of the Northamptonshire model maker W. J. Bassett-Lowke, and converted to 15-inch gauge. In this form it still exists, regrettably beyond the scope of this book.

Seen at Eskdale Green station, *Devon* was one of two Manning, Wardle 0-6-0Ts owned by the Ravenglass & Eskdale Railway. The tilt on the carriage next to the locomotive makes it look as though it has a broken spring.

SOUTHWOLD RAILWAY

A Southwold Railway ticket.

SOUTHWOLD RAILWAY.
Issued subject to Regulations in the
Company's Time Tables.
HALESWORTH
TO
SOUTHWOLD
THIRD CLASS   Fare 9d.

The Southwold Railway served a resort on the Suffolk coast, 8¾ miles from the market town of Halesworth, where it made a link with the Great Eastern Railway. Unusually, its construction was not motivated by the carriage of minerals. In addition to carrying passengers and goods, the railway's ability to carry fish enabled Southwold to compete with Lowestoft and other ports.

Authorised by an Act of Parliament in 1876, it was opened on 24 September 1879, when flooding at Wenhaston caused services to Halesworth to be suspended. Construction had been delayed by the difficulty in raising capital and acquiring the land and had been started only in June. The contractor was Charles Chambers, who in 1890 was to be engaged to rebuild the Potteries, Shrewsbury & North Wales Railway for the Shropshire Railways.

Sharp, Stewart supplied three 2-4-0Ts. Six tramcar-style carriages with Cleminson six-wheeled flexible underframes were obtained from the Bristol Wagon Works. Just short of Southwold the railway crossed the river Blythe on a swing bridge – an Admiralty requirement, despite the absence of vessels on the river.

An application to the Board of Trade for powers to raise additional capital was made in November 1879, but it took three more applications before

A mixed train at Southwold.

the required certificate was issued, in 1888. The railway paid its way and passenger numbers slowly increased.

The situation was sufficiently stable to consider expansion and in 1902 a Light Railway Order was made authorising an extension to Kessingland, Lowestoft, a distance of 9 miles. To facilitate the exchange of traffic with the Great Eastern Railway, it was to have been standard gauge; authority was given to convert the existing railway and to work it as a light railway as well. Several bridges, including the swing bridge, were altered to accommodate the wider gauge but lack of funding meant that the extension was not built.

A shorter, 1-mile extension was built to the harbour, an initiative of the Southwold Harbour Company, which obtained the necessary Light Railway Order in 1913. It was more steeply graded than the main line and a Manning, Wardle 0-6-2T was obtained to work it in 1914.

The First World War had a limited effect on the railway. There was troop traffic, some wagons were damaged by an incendiary bomb and the railway was used for the transportation of 680 Dutch passengers and seamen, who had been stranded in England by the war, to the harbour – the Germans guaranteed safe conduct only if Southwold was used. There were enough profits to pay a small dividend and to have the carriages overhauled.

In the late 1920s, competition from the buses increased, the weather was poor, and passenger numbers fell rapidly. The railway gained a reputation for the shambolic and bucolic way in which it was run, and two sets of postcards produced by a local artist illustrating it in this form found a ready

Southwold Railway Sharp, Stewart 2-4-0T No 3 *Blyth* at Southwold after 1900.

market. A writer in *The Times* said that the railway should not be mocked, for it had been the making of Southwold. After appeals for financial assistance failed, the last train ran on 11 April 1929, almost exactly fifty years after the first.

The company was put into receivership and the railway abandoned, left in limbo. The receiver could not dispose of the assets of a statutory company and there were no funds to apply for an abandonment order. In 1941 the assets were requisitioned for the war effort. All that was moveable had gone within a few months.

Owing to some judicial intransigence the company was left in suspense until 1992, when it was registered as a limited company under the Companies Act and finally liquidated. A society formed in 1994 to investigate the possibility of reviving the railway became a charitable trust in 2006. It is promoting the development of a railway centre at Wenhaston and the construction of a replica locomotive.

A Southwold Railway train arrives at Halesworth, the interchange station with the Great Eastern Railway.

THE LIGHT RAILWAYS

T HE LIGHT RAILWAYS ACT of 1896 was intended to simplify the process for
authorising a railway that might open up remote areas for development.
Instead of making an application to Parliament, the promoters would apply
to the Light Railway Commission, which would consider the application on
its merits and make a recommendation to the Board of Trade. Many orders
were made; not so many authorised lines were constructed. In the first flush
of enthusiasm after the Act came into effect there were four narrow gauge
light railways, with three different gauges.

VALE OF RHEIDOL LIGHT RAILWAY

The Vale of Rheidol Light Railway was the product of an 1897 Act of Parliament
that made use of provisions of the 1868 Regulation of Railways Act, which
imposed restrictions on axle loads, train speeds and level crossings. It had
a 12-mile route from the Cardigan Bay resort and fishing port of Aberystwyth,
up the Rheidol valley to Devil's Bridge. This was the centre of the local
road network that served a thinly spread community, and the location of a
300 foot waterfall that attracted significant numbers of tourists. A number
of ore mines were expected to provide traffic. One of the engineers, James
Weeks Szlumper, had been engineer of the North Wales Narrow Gauge
Railways since 1891 and the Lynton & Barnstaple Railway since 1895.

As was so often the case, capital was hard to come by and progress
was slow. A Light Railway Order was obtained for an extension to Aberayron
in 1898 and a second Act extended the time available for construction and
the authorised capital in 1900. The Pethick brothers of Plymouth started
construction in 1901 and the line was opened on 22 December 1902. Earlier
in the year a second Light Railway Order extended the time allowed for
building the Aberayron extension and authorised the working of the railway
as a light railway under the 1896 Act.

Davies & Metcalfe supplied two 2-6-2Ts, which proved to be capable
of the work expected of them. From 1903 they were supported by a
second-hand Bagnall 2-4-0T that had been built for export in 1896, sold

Opposite:
The longest of
the narrow gauge
light railways, a
Welsh Highland
Railway train
climbs through the
Aberglaslyn Pass
on its way to
Beddgelert and
Caernarfon. HM
the Queen and
HRH Prince Philip
travelled in the
observation car
between
Caernarfon and
Dinas on
27 April 2010.

Right: The first Aberystwyth terminus with the Swindon-built 2-6-2T No 7. In 1925 the Great Western Railway relocated the narrow gauge terminus to a new site alongside the standard gauge station.

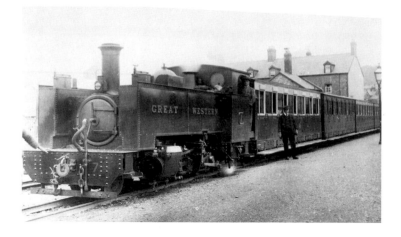

Right: The Vale of Rheidol Light Railway's company seal included an illustration of the Devil's Bridge in its design.

Below: A Vale of Rheidol Light Railway train at Aberystwyth shortly after the railway was opened.

to the nearby short-lived 2-foot 3-inch-gauge Plynlimon & Hafan Railway in 1897, and used (after re-gauging) by the contractors during the railway's construction. Twelve bogie carriages were obtained from the Midland Carriage & Wagon Company.

Construction cost more than the available capital and the contractors took control of the railway. From 1905 they made several attempts to sell it to the Cambrian Railways or the GWR and in 1910 a consortium of Cambrian directors took control, an arrangement that was regularised by legislation in 1913.

Notable features on the railway are the timber bridge crossing the river Rheidol, just over a mile from Aberystwyth, and the 1 in 50 gradient over the last 4 miles to Devil's Bridge. Traffic was a mixture of merchandise and passengers, with some minerals when the quarries were operating. In the summer the railway did well with tourists, but its big problem was that it tried to accommodate it all without adequate resources. For several summers from 1912 a locomotive had to be hired from the Festiniog Railway.

High up the Rheidol valley, the Bagnall 0-4-2T *Rheidol* rolls down the 1 in 50 gradient with a short train.

No 9 *Prince of Wales* taking water at Aberffrwd in 1961. The locomotive was built by the Great Western Railway in 1924. The passing loop was removed in 1963 and then reinstated by the present owners in 1990.

The BR blue livery applied in 1968 was not to everyone's taste but it was improved with the addition of lining and the brass double arrows.

Ownership changed again in 1922, when the Cambrian was absorbed by the GWR. This meant a new station at Aberystwyth, three new locomotives and sixteen new carriages. From 1931 the emphasis was on tourism, and the winter service was withdrawn.

British Railways took over on nationalisation in 1948 and, when steam was withdrawn from the national network in 1968, the VRLR became its last outpost in the state system. That year the narrow gauge station was relocated into the standard gauge station and the locomotives and carriages were housed in the standard gauge engine shed. They were also painted in corporate blue livery.

British Rail could not make the VRLR pay because the rail unions would not allow it to be treated as a tourist railway, with different conditions for the personnel concerned. A serious derailment at Nantyronen in 1986 showed that track maintenance left something to be desired. The idea of a sale had been mentioned in 1962 but it was not sold until March 1989, when it was purchased by the Brecon Mountain Railway, which continued to manage it until 1996. Ownership was transferred to a charitable trust in 1990 and the operating company became a charity in 1999.

In private ownership, most of the track has now been replaced with new materials; the river bridge has been replaced and two locomotives and fifteen carriages have been restored. The passing loops at Capel Bangor and Aberffrwd have been reinstated and a programme of station improvements

has been started. Construction of a lottery-supported workshop and engine shed was started in 2011.

Vale of Rheidol Light Railway No 8 (built by the Great Western Railway at Swindon in 1923) and its train wait to depart from Aberystwyth.

WELSHPOOL & LLANFAIR LIGHT RAILWAY

50 miles to the east of Aberystwyth, the Welshpool & Llanfair Light Railway was built with the aid of Treasury and local authority loans, which meant that, although it was owned by an independent company, it had to be built and operated by, in this case, the Cambrian Railways. It was the first

A typical Welshpool & Llanfair Light Railway train stands at Llanfair Caereinion with Beyer, Peacock 0-6-0T The Earl at its head. The only difference between the first- and third-class accommodation was the use of a piece of thin carpet as a seat cushion.

narrow gauge railway to be built using powers obtained under the 1896 Light Railways Act.

The 2-foot 6-inch-gauge track ran 9 miles westwards from a terminus opposite the Cambrian's station at Welshpool, terminating on the edge of the rural community of Llanfair Caereinion. Unlike the other Welsh narrow gauge lines, the imperative to build it came from agriculture, not the prospect of mineral traffic.

The Light Railway Order made in 1899 had taken more than two years to obtain and a second was required to increase the authorised capital before construction started. The line was opened for goods on 9 March 1903 and to passengers on 6 April of the same year. Beyer, Peacock supplied two sturdy 0-6-0T locomotives, and three bogie carriages with longitudinal seats were obtained from R.Y. Pickering. Most trains ran mixed.

At Welshpool, the line forged a sinuous route through the town, straddling the Lledan brook and crossing several roads before reaching open countryside at Raven Square. Notable features are the climb to Golfa, which includes a section of 1 in 29 (the steepest on any public railway in the United Kingdom), a stone viaduct at Brynelin, and the Banwy river bridge at Heniarth.

At opening, the railway was both under-capitalised and over-spent. The contractor's claim for £20,000 for extras went to arbitration, taking three years to resolve, although it was settled for £5,413. The railway was never debt-free,

One of the Welshpool & Llanfair Light Railway's original locomotives, Beyer, Peacock 0-6-0T *Countess*, restored to Great Western Railway condition and livery, with the railway's train of replica Pickering carriages at Raven Square station, Welshpool.

The Welshpool & Llanfair Light Railway's Kerr, Stuart 0-6-2T *Joan* worked in Antigua before being repatriated to the United Kingdom. Its train comprises the railway's two Hungarian bogie carriages.

owing £2,387 to the Cambrian by 31 December 1922. At the railway grouping in 1923, the GWR paid £20,000 for the railway and took on the debt.

The GWR rebuilt the locomotives at Swindon and withdrew the passenger service in 1931, the carriages going for scrap. British Railways obtained approval to close the railway in 1950 but ran it until 1956. Several 'farewell' excursions were run, with passengers riding in the coal wagons. Following

Ex-Sierra Leone Railway Hunslet 2-6-2T No 85 hauls a train of Austrian four-wheeled carriages on the Welshpool & Llanfair Light Railway.

Hauled by a Romanian 0-8-0T, the last train of the day returns to Llanfair Caereinion, the Welshpool & Llanfair Light Railway's headquarters.

the examples of the Talyllyn and Festiniog Railways, a preservation society was formed, taking over the railway – except the town section – in 1963.

The sixtieth anniversary of the opening was marked by the restoration of services between Llanfair Caereinion and Castle Caereinion. The original locomotives had been bought from BR and carriages obtained from the Admiralty. The first years were difficult, especially after the Banwy bridge was undermined by scouring in December 1964, but gradually the railway found its feet, extending back to Castle Caereinion in 1965, to Sylfaen in 1972 and to Raven Square, on the edge of Welshpool, in 1981.

For additional locomotives and rolling stock, the line looked overseas, acquiring locomotives from Austria, Antigua, Sierra Leone, Finland and Romania and carriages from Austria, Sierra Leone and Hungary, giving the railway a very distinctive appearance.

A lottery-supported project included the re-boiling of the original locomotives in time for their centenary in 2003. The last of three replica Pickering carriages built by the Festiniog Railway was delivered in 2010.

LEEK & MANIFOLD LIGHT RAILWAY
In a remote area of North Staffordshire, the Leek & Manifold Light Railway was also 2-foot 6-inch gauge and built with the aid of public loans. Running between Waterhouses and Hulme End, a distance of 8½ miles, it was operated by the North Staffordshire Railway.

After two years of planning, in 1899 the relevant Light Railway Order authorised two railways, a standard gauge branch of the North Staffordshire Railway from Cheddleton, near Leek, to Waterhouses (9¾ miles), and its narrow gauge continuation into the Manifold valley. The latter was to be built and maintained by the Leek & Manifold Valley Light Railway Company.

Construction was started in 1902, taking just over two years. The line was built to principles developed by E. R. Calthrop, an engineer with advanced ideas on light railways and how they should be built to maximise efficiency. The best compromise between economy of construction and capacity, he argued, was 2-foot 6-inch gauge. All vehicles, including locomotives, should have the same axle loading to permit the maximum loading of goods wagons – 5 tons, allowing the use of rails weighing 30 pounds per yard. His ideas were showcased on the Indian Barsi Light Railway, which had opened in 1897. He had also been consulted during the planning stages of the Welshpool & Llanfair Light Railway.

Calthrop's influence was demonstrated in the design of the two Kitson 2-6-4T locomotives and the four open saloon carriages with gangways and open balconies, built in Preston. Most stations had a short length of standard gauge track to accommodate vehicles carried on transporter wagons. The locomotives were painted brown and the carriages primrose yellow.

The line meandered through the Manifold valley, a popular tourist destination which brought the railway most of its passengers, the local

The area around Thor's Cave in the Manifold Valley remains as popular with tourists now as it was when served by a narrow gauge railway.

More than any other, this photograph of a Leek & Manifold Light Railway train in the Manifold valley epitomises the splendour of the location.

communities being thinly spread. Simply, the gradient profile was 'V' shaped, the line falling to Grindon from either end; the steepest section was a short 1 in 40 near Waterhouses. The tunnel at Swainley, near Hulme End, is 164 yards long.

A Leek & Manifold Light Railway train at Hulme End. A van has been loaded on to a transporter wagon coupled next to the locomotive. The building with the curved roof is the engine shed.

The North Staffordshire Railway did much to publicise the Manifold valley and its railway, commissioning photographs and publishing several coloured picture postcards to promote them. On bank holidays, traffic was so heavy that every vehicle was pressed into use, passengers even riding on the transporter wagons. The main cargo, however, was milk, and traffic increased substantially when a new dairy was opened at Ecton, 7¼ miles from Waterhouses, in 1918. Its closure in 1932 precipitated the railway's closure the following year, after thirty years of use. In common with the other light railways already described, the LMVLR was saddled with construction debt that it was unable to pay off. At the railway grouping in 1923 the London, Midland & Scottish Railway had acquired the line for just short of £30,000, less than half of its £68,000 capital expenditure. There was little incentive to keep the railway open once the main traffic had gone.

The line was demolished in 1937 and its trackbed donated to Staffordshire County Council. As it was cleared it was converted into a footpath, now called the Manifold Way. Motor vehicles were given access to a 2-mile section, including the tunnel, in 1952. The Hulme End station building was restored as a visitor centre in 1997 and the Waterhouses signal box is preserved at the Amerton Railway near Uttoxeter.

CAMPBELTOWN & MACHRIHANISH LIGHT RAILWAY

Knowledge of the coalfield on the Kintyre peninsula, on Scotland's Argyll coast, is not widely held nowadays. The 2-foot 3-inch-gauge railway developed to serve it, from 1877 onwards, became Scotland's only public narrow gauge railway, the Campbeltown & Machrihanish Light Railway.

At Campbeltown's Old Quay on the Kintyre peninsular, a heavy Campbeltown & Machrihanish Light Railway train waits for its passengers, who have travelled down the Clyde, to finish boarding.

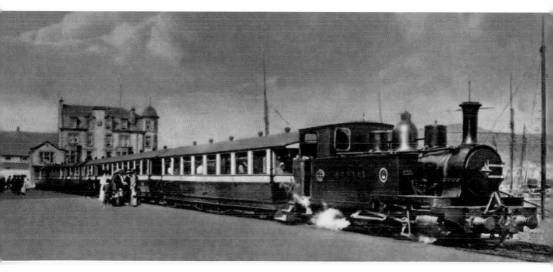

The guard and fireman pose with their train at Machrihanish.

The railway ran east–west across the Kintyre peninsula for about 5 miles and had two steam locomotives. Although some coal was exported, most was consumed locally, so demand for it was seasonal. As Campbeltown was a popular tourist destination for visitors travelling by ferry from Glasgow, the colliery company registered the Argyll Railway Company and applied for a Light Railway Order that was made in 1905.

To accommodate passenger trains, the mineral railway was rebuilt with modifications in some places that made it slightly over 5 miles long. At Campbeltown it ran as a street tramway on to the wharf. The train service started in August 1906, just in time for the tourists.

Two of the colliery locomotives were retained to deal with the coal traffic, one of them having vacuum brakes fitted to enable its use with light passenger trains. Two handsome Barclay 0-6-2Ts were bought for the ordinary passenger service. Pickering supplied six 43-foot-long bogie carriages, larger versions of those previously supplied to the Welshpool & Llanfair Light Railway.

In common with most of the other railways accounted for here, the CMLR was a victim of the inter-war Depression and competition from motor transport. There was no joy to be had from the operation of two motorbuses purchased to augment the train service, and in 1932 the want of repairs to the steam locomotives brought an end to the railway. A winding-up order was obtained in November 1933 and the railway was dismantled by a scrap merchant in 1934.

BETWEEN THE WARS: A NARROW GAUGE SWANSONG

DURING THE 1920s a small revival in the promotion of narrow gauge light railways produced two lines with very different characteristics.

WELSH HIGHLAND RAILWAY

Opened between Porthmadog and Dinas in 1923, the Welsh Highland Railway united two railways and saw trains running through the Aberglaslyn Pass after many years' anticipation.

The railways united were the North Wales Narrow Gauge Railways, already encountered, and the Portmadoc, Beddgelert & South Snowdon Railway. The latter's proposal was to make railways from Borth y Gest,

A busy scene at Beddgelert on the Welsh Highland Railway, with Hunslet 2-6-2T *Russell* (left) and the Baldwin. The first had been altered in a vain attempt to make it fit the Festiniog Railway loading gauge.